ANIMAL KINGDOM CLASSIFICATION

STARFISH, URCHINS & OTHER
ECHINODERMS

By Daniel Gilpin

Content Adviser: Leonard Muscatine, Ph.D.,
Emeritus Professor of Biology,
University of California, Los Angeles

Science Adviser: Terrence E. Young Jr., M.Ed., M.L.S.,
Jefferson (Louisiana) Public School System

First published in the United States in 2006 by
Compass Point Books
3109 West 50th St., #115
Minneapolis, MN 55410

ANIMAL KINGDOM CLASSIFICATION–ECHINODERMS
was produced by

David West Children's Books
7 Princeton Court
55 Felsham Road
London SW15 1AZ

Designer: David West
Editors: Gail Bushnell, Anthony Wacholtz, Kate Newport
Page Production: James Mackey

Visit Compass Point Books on the Internet at
www.compasspointbooks.com
or e-mail your request to
custserv@compasspointbooks.com

Library of Congress Cataloging-in-Publication Data
Gilpin, Daniel.
  Starfish, urchins & other echinoderms / by Daniel Gilpin.
    p. cm.— (Animal kingdom classification)
  Includes bibliographical references.
  ISBN 0-7565-1611-0 (hard cover)
 1. Echinodermata—Juvenile literature. 2. Starfishes—Juvenile literature. 3. Sea urchins—Juvenile literature. I. Title: Starfish, urchins, and other echinoderms. II. Title. III. Series.
  QL381.G55 2006
  593.9—dc22   2005029184

PHOTO CREDITS:
Abbreviations: t-top, m-middle, b-bottom, r-right,
l-left, c-center.

Title page, NOAA; 4/5, Dr. Aleksey Zuyev, NOAA; 9b, Steve McWilliam, iStockphoto.com; 10, Kip Evens, NOAA; 11l, OAR/National Undersea Research Program (NURP); 11t, Dr. Aleksey Zuyev, NOAA; 11b, OAR/National Undersea Research Program (NURP); 12, Dr. James P. McVey, NOAA; 13, Oxford Scientific Films; 14l, Oxford Scientific Films; 14r, Andrew Dean, iStockphoto.com; 15, Oxford Scientific Films; 17, Oxford Scientific Films; 18b, Dr. James P. McVey, NOAA; 18t, Oxford Scientific Films; 19l, Oxford Scientific Films; 19t, Dr. James P. McVey, NOAA; 20t, Paul Wolf, iStockphoto.com; 20b, Oxford Scientific Films; 21t, Dr. James P. McVey, NOAA; 21m, Dr. James P. McVey, NOAA; 21b, Oxford Scientific Films; 22/23(all), Oxford Scientific Films; 24/24, Yuri A. Zuyev, NOAA; 25m, NOAA; 25b, Dr. James P. McVey, NOAA; 26/27, OAR/National Undersea Research Program (NURP); 27t, Oxford Scientific Films; 28t, Florida Keys National Marine Sanctuary; 28b, Oxford Scientific Films; 29l, Oxford Scientific Films; 31b, OAR/National Undersea Research Program (NURP); 32t, Dr. James P. McVey, NOAA; 32b, Oxford Scientific Films; 33t, NOAA; 33l, NOAA; 33r, Dr. James P. McVey, NOAA; 34t, Goh Siang, iStockphoto.com; 35t,m,bl, Dr. James P. McVey, NOAA; 35br, Jeffrey Hochstrasser, iStockphoto.com; 36b, Oxford Scientific Films; 37tl, Oxford Scientific Films; 37tr, OAR/National Undersea Research Program (NURP); 37b, Oxford Scientific Films; 38/39, Oxford Scientific Films; 38, Dan Scmitt, iStockphoto.com; 39t, Oxford Scientific Films; 40/41, Oxford Scientific Films; 41t, The Natural History Museum, London; 41b, Oxford Scientific Films; 42, Carl Kehlenbach, iStockphoto.com; 43t, William B. Folsom NMFS, NOAA; 43m, Sergey Kashkin, iStockphoto.com; 43br, NOAA; 43bl, Dr. James P. McVey, NOAA

Every effort has been made to contact copyright holders of any material reproduced in this book. Any omissions will be rectified in subsequent printings if notice is given to the publishers.

With special thanks to the models: Felix Blom, Tucker Bryant, and Margaux Monfared.

Front cover: Starfish
Opposite: Starfish

ANIMAL KINGDOM CLASSIFICATION

STARFISH, URCHINS & OTHER
ECHINODERMS

Daniel Gilpin

COMPASS POINT BOOKS ✦ MINNEAPOLIS, MINNESOTA

TABLE OF CONTENTS

INTRODUCTION

To most of us, echinoderms are mysterious animals, yet they include some of the most common creatures on Earth. In many parts of the deep sea, they are the most abundant animals, sometimes covering the seabed. The reason we find echinoderms so mysterious is because there are no land echinoderms at all, nor are there any that live in freshwater. Nearly all species live in the deep ocean, although some can survive in brackish, or part salty, water. As adults, none of them are active swimmers, and most spend their lives fixed to one spot or slowly creeping over the sea bottom.

When still, many feather stars look like plants. These echinoderms have feathery arms, hence the name. They are the red-colored creatures in this picture, sitting on the coral. Some feather stars have as few as five arms, and others have as many as 200.

TYPES OF ECHINODERMS

Echinoderms include some of Earth's strangest animals. In fact, many of them do not even look like animals at all. The echinoderms are an ancient group, which partly explains their alien appearance. There were once more than 20 different classes. Today, only five remain.

ARMY OF ARMS
Three of the living echinoderm classes have arms: the starfish, brittle stars, and crinoids, which include feather stars and sea lilies. In all of these groups, the arms are arranged around a central body. In most species, the body is smaller than the limbs themselves. The arms are used for movement and feeding. Most have tube feet, controlled by an internal hydraulic system.

CROWNING GLORY

Feather stars sift tiny food particles from the water with their fringed arms. The smaller projections underneath are used for moving and gripping to rocks.

ROUGH STUFF

Starfish have a solid appearance with no obvious dividing line between their arms and body. The undersides of the arms are covered with numerous tube feet. The top of the animal usually has a rough texture.

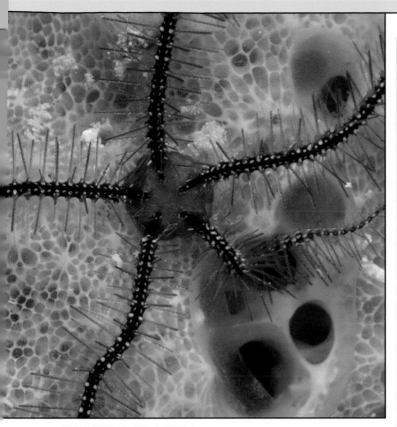

FRAGILE BEAUTY

Brittle stars have very long, thin arms, which they wriggle to move quickly along. Unlike starfish, the disk-shaped body is quite distinct. The brittle star (above) is clambering over a sponge.

SAUSAGES AND SPINES

The other two classes of living echinoderms contain the sea cucumbers and sea urchins. Sea cucumbers are the only echinoderms with elongated bodies. They move by means of tube feet, which are concentrated on the underside. They also have other, larger tube feet around their mouths that have evolved into specialized feeding structures. Sea urchins have oval, ball-shaped, or disk-shaped bodies that are covered with spines. Most live on the seabed, although a few spend their lives buried in soft sediment. Sea urchins feed on both algae and animal matter. They grind up their food using a hard structure called the "Aristotle's lantern," a complex arrangement of skeletal elements and teeth.

SUSPENSION FEEDER

Some sea cucumbers use their feeding tube feet to capture food particles from the water and pass them to the mouth.

INSIDE OUT

A walk along the beach often turns up sea urchin remains. The rounded "shells," or tests, survive long after the flesh has rotted and the spines have washed away. Sea urchin tests are made up of fused plates of calcium carbonate just beneath the skin. In life, they contain all of the internal organs.

These tests were collected on a beach.

WHERE ECHINODERMS LIVE

All echinoderms live in salty water. A few inhabit estuaries, mouths of rivers big enough for tides to flow in, and some hide in submarine sand or mud. Most however, live on the seabed creeping along in search of food or waiting for food to come to them.

IN THE SHALLOWS

The place most of us see echinoderms is at the beach. Starfish, sea urchins, and sea cucumbers sometimes become trapped in tide pools. Unable to leave the water, they are forced to stay until the tide comes back in and floods the pools, enabling them to escape.

Many echinoderms live on the seafloor at various depths but some are restricted to the shallows because that is where their food lives. The crown-of-thorns starfish, for example, feeds on coral, most of which is found only in shallow tropical and subtropical waters.

WARM WATERS

Some echinoderms, such as this cushion star, live on coral reefs in shallow seas. These coastal habitats usually support a great abundance of life.

DARK AND DEEP

In many ways, the seabed is the echinoderms' kingdom. Huge numbers of them live there, many in very deep waters. Although some echinoderms have simple eyelike structures that can detect light, they rely mainly on touch to find their way around. For this reason, the darkness of the deep sea is not a disadvantage to them. They thrive in conditions in which many other animals would not survive.

STUCK IN THE MUD

Although most echinoderms live on the seabed, some live in it, burrowing into the sediment. Some sea cucumbers do this, living a bit like earthworms on land. They swallow the sand or mud, digest the nutrients in it, and excrete the rest. Other burrowers, such as sand dollars, dig to feed and hide.

DISTANT RELATIVES

Starfish and sea urchins (above), are both echinoderms. Although they look very different, they have similar lifestyles, wandering slowly over the seabed in search of food.

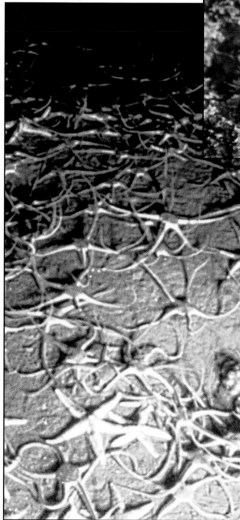

CARPET OF STARS

Far below the waves, the floor of the deep sea is prime echinoderm habitat. Most of the creatures in this picture are brittle stars.

FEELING THE HEAT

Echinoderms survive in the most incredible places. Some live below the ice of the Arctic Ocean, while others inhabit the waters around hydrothermal vents on the seafloor. These submarine geysers pump out scalding water heated by molten rock just under Earth's crust. The brittle stars and other echinoderms that live here avoid entering the boiling plumes but can tolerate much higher temperatures than most sea life.

A hydrothermal vent

FEATURES OF AN ECHINODERM

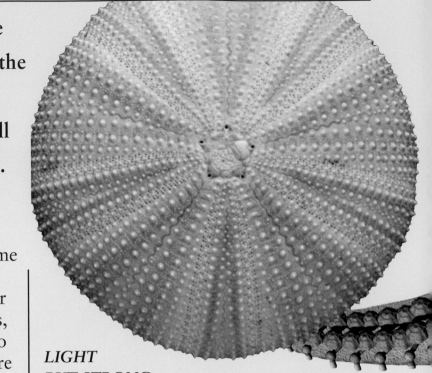

Echinoderms are unique in the animal kingdom. They are the only creatures with bodies built with a five-sectioned structure. All echinoderms have this basic form.

BUNCH OF FIVES

Echinoderms form five classes in the animal kingdom, but their bodies come in three main shapes. The first is the star shape, with the "rays" of the star formed by arms. Starfish, brittle stars, feather stars, and sea lilies all fall into this category. In sea lilies, the arms are used solely for feeding. The spiny ball is the second shape, seen in sea urchins. The third shape is the elongated body, as seen in the sea cucumbers. They are also built on a five-section plan.

LIGHT BUT STRONG

When sea urchins die, their spines and soft tissues fall away. What is left is a rounded shell, or "test," formed from chalky plates that were once in the animal's skin. The sea urchin's five-point symmetry is shown on the top and bottom of these tests.

SEA URCHIN

Most sea urchins are covered by protective spines. They are hinged at the base and help the animal move. The tube feet play an even bigger part in movement. Alone, they look small and weak, but together they form a powerful unit.

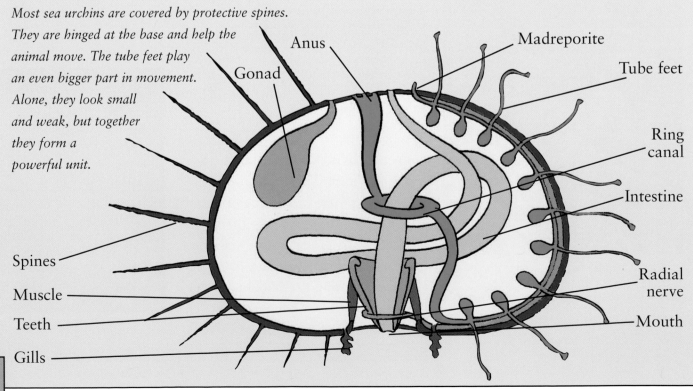

Anus
Gonad
Madreporite
Tube feet
Ring canal
Intestine
Radial nerve
Mouth
Spines
Muscle
Teeth
Gills

Stomach

A starfish's mouth is in the center of its body, on its underside. Some starfish draw food into the mouth, passing particles toward it with the tube feet. Others extend their stomach out of their mouth to engulf prey. Waste is expelled through the anus on the top of the body.

Gonads

These paired organs are held in the starfish's arms. They produce the eggs or sperm that the animal uses for breeding. Echinoderms are either male or female.

Ring Canal

Starfish move by hydraulics. Muscles push water from the central ring through canals that run down each arm, branching off to the tube feet.

NEW FROM OLD

Starfish have incredible powers of regeneration. If they lose a limb to a predator, they soon grow another one. Even more remarkably, a whole starfish can grow from one arm, provided some of the central disk remains attached to it. The new animal is a genetic clone of the arm's original owner, so the process can be considered an extreme version of asexual reproduction.

A lost arm sprouts new limbs.

Suckers

Each of the many tube feet on the underside of a starfish's arms, ends in a tiny suction cup. These help the starfish to move along and grip prey. They contract, forming suction, when water is drawn out of them.

Gut Pouch

Tubes extend from the stomach to pouches in each of the arms. These break food down further, and pass nutrients through their walls to be transported around the body.

Pedicellaria

Madreporite

Gills

Spine

STARFISH SKIN

All echinoderms, including starfish, have chalky plates or spines in their skin. Pedicellaria are tiny pincers that keep the skin free of parasites. Madreporites let water enter the hydraulic system.

ORIGINS OF ECHINODERMS

Echinoderms are ancient animals. The group's oldest fossils date back 600 million years. However, the origins of echinoderms are mysterious and their ancestors unknown.

HARD EVIDENCE

Fossils show that all of the modern echinoderm groups had appeared by about 400 million years ago. Because they have hard parts in their bodies, echinoderms form good fossils, which can be easily identified by comparing them with living examples.

SEA URCHIN

Fossils (above) show how sea urchins have barely changed in millions of years. The earliest known sea urchin fossil is around 450 million years old.

LONG LOST RELATIVES

Many ancient types of echinoderms are now extinct. Living echinoderms are grouped into five classes, but paleontologists have identified at least 17 more classes that no longer exist. Edrioasteroids, for example, looked like starfish but lived attached to the bottom by a short, thick stalk.

PERFECT EXAMPLE

As their name suggests, brittle stars break easily, so complete fossils of them are rare.

FIVE FROM TWO

Although the ancestry of today's echinoderms is unknown, we do know that they evolved from creatures with bilateral, or two-way, symmetry rather than pentaradial, or five-way, symmetry. Scientists know this because the larvae of living echinoderms are bilaterally symmetrical, which means a line can be drawn down the middle to show two halves that are mirror images of each other.

ORDOVICIAN OCEAN

More than 200 million years before the first dinosaurs, echinoderms already filled the seas. An illustration shows the brittle star Lapworthia, clambering over delicate Eucalyptocrinites sea lilies, while stocky sea lilies grow in the background.

1. *Eucalyptocrinite*
2. *Sea lilies*
3. *Starfish*
4. *Sea urchin*
5. *Brittle star*

LILY GARDEN

Sea lilies were once much more common than they are today. Fossils (right) show that in some places, they virtually covered the sea bottom, forming huge submarine "gardens." Sea lilies dominated much of the ocean until around 245 million years ago, when the vast majority of species, including the dinosaurs, suddenly became extinct.

Fossilized sea lilies can sometimes be found in large numbers.

GETTING AROUND

Most echinoderms travel slowly, and some spend their adult lives anchored to one spot. Only brittle stars are capable of rapid motion. Most others get around using their spines or tube feet.

ON TIPTOES
Starfish can move all of their arms at once if necessary, lifting their bodies right up off the seabed.

SLOW BUT SURE
Starfish, sea cucumbers, and sea urchins travel so gradually that they often hardly seem to be moving at all. These creatures all have tube feet. Starfish and sea cucumbers move by means of these alone. Sea urchins also use their tube feet to get around, but most do so with the added help of their spines, which can be moved individually. Feather stars have projections off their undersides called cirri. These move independently, enabling them to creep along. Some feather stars can also swim by undulating their feathery arms.

HOW TUBE FEET WORK

Tube feet extend from beneath a starfish's arm.

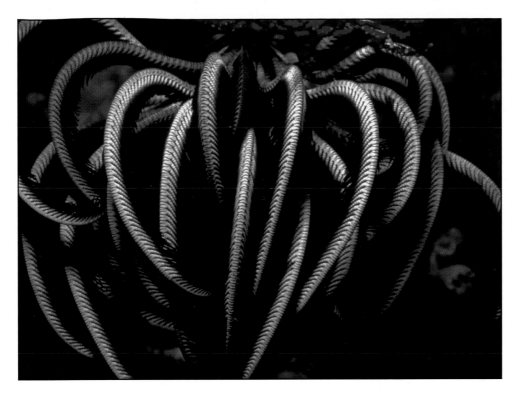

POETRY IN MOTION

Most echinoderms never leave the seafloor, but many feather stars can swim. This ability helps these delicate creatures escape predators. Feather stars evolved from sea lilies, which can neither crawl nor swim.

GOING NOWHERE

Travel is not an option for sea lilies. As adults, they live firmly attached to one spot. Sea lilies are held to the seabed by a long stalk with two parts, the columnal and the holdfast. The columnal is a long, slender structure, strong enough to lift the main body of the animal off the bottom and flexible enough to move with currents in the water. The holdfast links the columnal to the bottom. It has a branching structure similar to the roots of a plant. Sea lilies' arms are used entirely for feeding and are flexible like those of their cousins, the feather stars.

SPEED DEMONS

Brittle stars are the sprinters of the echinoderm world. They travel by bending and flexing their arms to pull themselves over the seabed, moving much faster than other echinoderms. Some brittle stars can wriggle their arms quick enough to actually lift themselves off the seabed and swim. This allows them to escape from predators, such as crabs.

Tube feet are unique to echinoderms. They are operated by changes in water pressure in channels inside the animal, combined with muscle movement. As water is forced into a tube foot by the contraction of a muscular sac above it, it extends. Other tiny muscles control the direction in which it extends. Starfish and sea cucumbers move by extending and contracting all their tube feet with a rippling motion. Suction caps at the end of each tube foot give the animal its grip.

BETWEEN THE SPINES

The tube feet of sea urchins have to be long enough to extend beyond their spines. Both the tube feet and spines are used for movement.

FOOD AND FEEDING

Echinoderms feed in a variety of ways. Some swallow sand and sediment from the seafloor, digesting the organic matter within it. Some are suspension feeders, sifting tiny organisms from the water. Others are scavengers or even predators that hunt live prey.

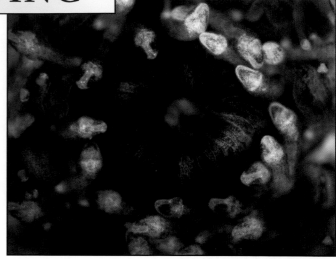

The mouths are usually centered on the underside of most echinoderms, but are on the top of sea lilies. Sea urchins move food to the mouth by tube feet and pedicellaria (above).

VACUUMING UP FOOD

Most sea cucumbers feed by sucking up sediment from the seabed. The particles of dead plant or animal matter in it are then digested, along with any tiny living creatures, and the gritty remains are expelled as waste. Heart urchins, or sea potatoes, plow through the sediment to find their food. They pick out edible particles using their tube feet.

Not all sea cucumbers get their food from sediment. Some are suspension feeders with feathery tentacles (left) around their mouths.

18

The crown-of-thorns starfish specializes in eating coral. In recent years, it has earned a bad reputation, causing plagues that have killed whole sections of reef. Some scientists believe the decline of the giant triton, the crown-of-thorns' main predator, is the cause of this because it has been almost wiped out by shell collectors.

The crown-of-thorns is covered with venomous spines.

DEADLY GRIP

Many starfish hunt bivalve mollusks. They pull the two halves of the shell apart, then force their stomach in through the gap to digest their prey.

HUNTING PREY

Starfish are mainly carnivorous animals. Some scavenge, seeking out dead creatures on the seabed, but others are active hunters. Slow movers, starfish mainly hunt animals that cannot escape. Bivalve mollusks, such as clams, are among the favorite prey of many species. Their shells provide little defense against a starfish's powerful arms. Other prey includes sea squirts and sponges, which live attached to corals and rocks.

SIFTED MEALS

Sea lilies and feather stars feed on the tiny algae and animals that make up plankton. They catch these tiny organisms with their outstretched, feathery arms, known as pinnules. Each pinnule is coated with a sticky mucuslike substance, which traps the plankton. The food is then gradually moved toward the central mouth by means of tiny tube feet. Some brittle stars also filter feed in a similar way.

STICKY TRAP

Feather stars collect planktonic organisms and other floating particles of food with their arms, which are known as pinnules.

ATTACK AND DEFENSE

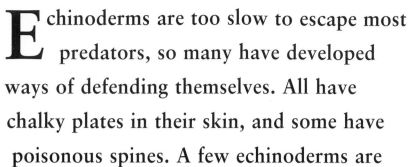

Echinoderms are too slow to escape most predators, so many have developed ways of defending themselves. All have chalky plates in their skin, and some have poisonous spines. A few echinoderms are predators themselves, with their own methods of attacking prey.

DIE HARDS

The word *echinoderm* literally means "spiny skin." The chalky nodules, spikes, and plates that give them their name make them hard to kill and unpleasant to eat. A few creatures prey on echinoderms despite their defenses, but they usually prefer to hunt animals that are easier to digest. One animal that does hunt them is the sea otter. It dives for sea urchins, which it brings to the surface. Lying on its back, it smashes them open against pebbles on its chest.

NOT FUSSY

Seagulls will eat almost anything they can find on the beach, including starfish. Tough, gritty skin is no protection against these adaptable birds.

LEAVE ME ALONE!

Sea cucumbers have one of the strangest defense mechanisms in the animal kingdom. When they are provoked, they shoot threads of material from their anus or exit hole. These are strong and sticky enough to disable most attackers, or at least distract them so that the sea cucumber can escape. Sea cucumbers fire these threads as a last resort. Once they have been shot out, they cannot be drawn back in. However, they are slowly regenerated inside the animal.

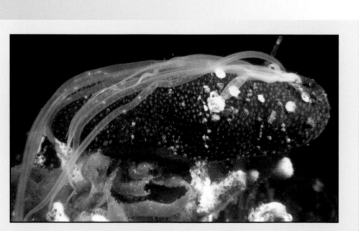

This sea cucumber has fired its threads.

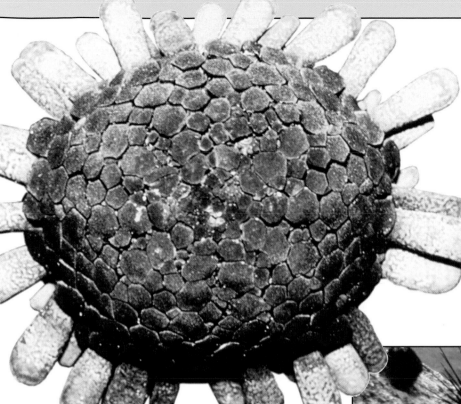

LITTLE TANK

Shingle urchins (left) live in shallow coastal waters and have tough body armor to protect them from predators.

MAKING A POINT

Sea urchins are perhaps the best-protected echinoderms of all. Their spines keep most predators away from their bodies, which are themselves encased inside solid tests. The sharp spines of many sea urchins break off easily, embedding themselves in the skin of careless attackers.

WELL PROTECTED

Some sea urchins are protected by very long spines. Between these are pincerlike pedicellaria, which can be poisonous and are used for defense.

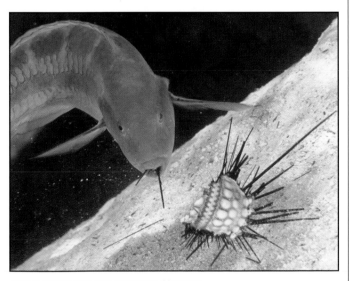

PERSISTENT PREDATOR

With their tough, horny beaks, parrotfish are among the few animals that prey on sea urchins.

ON THE HUNT

Predatory starfish attack and kill slowly. The creatures they eat are even less mobile than they are, so catching them is simply a matter of finding them on the seabed. Bivalve mollusks are pried open and digested alive, the starfish slipping its stomach between the two halves of its prey's shell and over the soft flesh inside. Some starfish graze on coral polyps and other small animals, similar to the way some sea urchins feed on algae.

21

Echinoderms reproduce in a number of ways. All reproduce sexually, the females producing eggs and the males producing sperm. Some can split to form two new individuals, a form of asexual reproduction.

SEA URCHIN LARVAE

Newly hatched pluteus larvae look like little arrowheads. As they grow, they change into miniature adults (left) before settling on the seabed.

TWO SYSTEMS

Most echinoderms are either male or female. During the spawning season, which varies between species, the females produce large numbers of eggs and release them into the water. This triggers the males to release sperm. The eggs and sperm mingle in the water and the eggs become fertilized.

Some starfish and sea cucumbers can also reproduce asexually, splitting off parts of their bodies to form new individuals.

SPAWNING SEA URCHINS

In echinoderms, eggs and sperm mix outside the body. Many are washed away before they can meet, so these creatures produce huge numbers of both.

TINY LIVES

Fertilized echinoderm eggs develop and hatch out as larvae. Echinoderm larvae look very different from their parents. For a start, their bodies have two distinct halves that are mirror images of each other. The typical five-part echinoderm structure develops later as the larvae grow and change.

Newly hatched echinoderm larvae have distinct forms, which vary from class to class. Starfish hatch into larvae known as bipinnaria. These grow into slightly more complex brachiolaria before undergoing a complete transformation into the adult form.

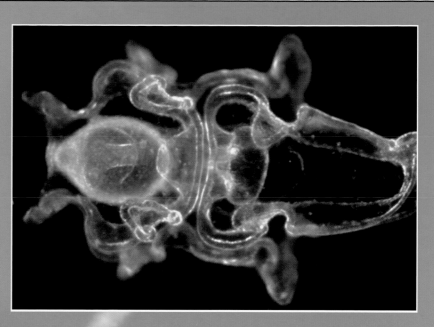

STARFISH BIPINNARIA LARVAE

Most echinoderm larvae live as free-swimming organisms in the plankton. Most move by means of tiny hairlike structures called cilia, which beat rhythmically and cover their bodies.

SETTLING DOWN

As planktonic echinoderm larvae start to change into their adult form, they tend to seek out others of their own kind before settling. For a long time, it was not known how they did this, but recent studies suggest that they follow trails of pheromones given off by the adults. In some species, the actual process of metamorphosis from larval to adult forms is triggered by these chemicals.

When they become adults, sea urchins often form big colonies and live close to each other.

STARFISH

Starfish are the most familiar echinoderms to most people. Their unique shape makes them easy to identify and separate from other sea creatures. Most starfish have five thick arms, but some have more.

A CLASS OF THEIR OWN

Starfish make up one of the five classes of living echinoderms, the class Asteroidea, which literally means "the star-shaped ones." There are around 1,800 known species in the class, and there are probably more in the deep sea that have yet to be discovered.

Starfish live on the seabed and are found in all of the world's oceans. Many prey on mollusks such as clams and oysters and are considered pests by people who harvest these shellfish for a living. Most starfish are either predators or scavengers, although some feed on microscopic organisms, which they pass to the mouth using their tube feet.

RED STAR

Many starfish are richly colored. Often, different individuals from the same species have different shades. The reason for this variety is unclear since starfish have simple eyes and cannot see color.

TOUGH CUSTOMER

Some starfish have body armor to protect them from predators. Most species have small plates of calcium carbonate in their skin, but a few have developed scutes, or thick lumps. The giant spined sea star from the western Pacific is one such creature. Its pointed scutes actually stick out through its skin like spikes, making it a challenge for even the toughest of predators.

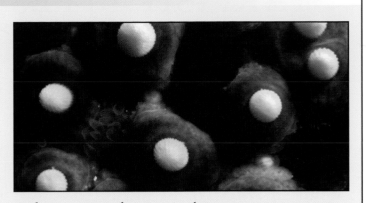

A close-up view of giant spined sea star scutes

A LIVING CONSTELLATION

Starfish sometimes gather in large numbers. They are drawn together by food or the urge to breed.

ALL ARMS

Like all echinoderms, starfish have bodies split into five different sections. Most starfish have a single arm protruding from each of these sections, although some have two per section and others as many as eight. A few starfish break the general rule by having six, seven, 11, or 24 arms altogether, meaning that some sections have more arms on them than others.

ROUNDED INDIVIDUALS

In most starfish, the arms make up the bulk of the animal's weight. Cushion stars, however, have short stubby arms, and a few have no arms at all. Their rounded shape makes it hard for cushion stars to lever shellfish open. Instead most feed on easier prey, such as sponges.

BIG BLOOM

Sunflower starfish can have up to 24 arms and reach over 3 feet (.9 m) across.

CUSHION STAR

Some cushion stars look like spineless sea urchins. Despite their appearance, they are actually starfish.

STARFISH TYPES

In animal classification, starfish have a whole class to themselves, just like birds, mammals, and reptiles do. Within that class, Asteroidea, there is surprising variety. Starfish come in a huge range of colors, shapes, sizes, and forms.

PROTECTIVE LUMPS
The calcium carbonate plates in their skin make many starfish appear warty. These lumps are hard and protect the starfish from attack.

LOTS OF LIMBS

Ask people to draw a starfish and most will come up with a five-armed creature. While most starfish do have five arms, many species have more. Sun stars can have as many as 24. The crown-of-thorns starfish also has many arms, sometimes as many as 21. They both start adult life with five and grow more as they mature.

Starfish can easily regenerate lost arms. Occasionally, two arms will grow from the point where just one was lost. As a result, some starfish, from species normally described as having five arms, actually have six or seven.

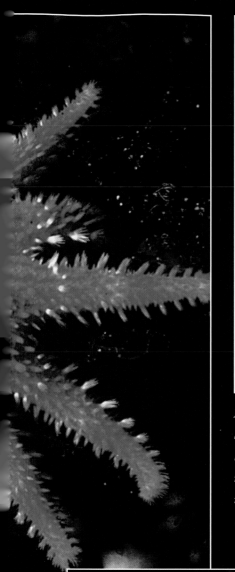

INSIDES OUT

Many starfish evert their stomachs to feed (right). This enables them to hunt creatures that would otherwise be impossible to eat. Bivalve shellfish, such as oysters, are too well protected for most other invertebrates to attack. Starfish digest them by pulling their shells slightly open and forcing their everted stomachs through, releasing digestive juices directly on to their prey.

A starfish everts its stomach.

ARMS LIKE RAYS

Sun stars can grow quite large. The biggest species may have arm spans of more than 3 feet (.9 m) across.

ALL IN ORDER

The class Asteroidea is split into seven different orders: Brisingida, Forcipulatida, Notomyotida, Paxillosida, Spinulosida, Valvatida, and Velatida. Scientists separate them by subtle differences in body structures. For instance, members of the order Forcipulatida have pedicellaria shaped like forceps. To the untrained eye, these differences can be hard to spot.

LONG AND SMOOTH

Not all starfish have rough skin. As invertebrates, starfish are not true fish at all. Some scientists prefer to call them sea stars.

WELL ROUNDED

Cushion stars have thick bodies with arms linked by folds of flesh. There are many species, some of which have no arms at all.

BRITTLE STARS

At first sight, brittle stars look like starfish. Closer inspection, however, shows them to be quite different. Unlike starfish, they have thin, agile arms and can move quickly.

ON THE GO

Brittle stars move by wriggling their arms, which are clearly separated from their disklike, armored bodies. Starfish, on the other hand, can only travel by means of their tube feet and move very slowly. Each brittle star arm is supported by an internal skeleton of calcium carbonate, made up of numerous plates known as vertebral ossicles. These are connected together with ball and socket joints and make the arms extremely flexible.

BRIGHT AND BEAUTIFUL

Many brittle stars are drab-looking animals, but some, particularly on reefs, are brightly colored. Brittle stars range greatly in size. The arms of the largest species may reach 2 feet (0.6 m) long.

CLIMBING FRAME

Brittle stars can use their arms to grip and wrap around objects to move around. As their name suggests, their arms can break off easily.

WRITHING MASS
Brittle stars are extremely numerous, sometimes forming swarms that coat the seafloor.

TRIBAL GATHERING

Brittle stars and the larger, lesser known basket stars make up the class Ophiuroidea, one of the five classes of living echinoderms. There are around 1,600 known species in the class altogether. They live throughout the world's oceans, from Arctic and Antarctic waters to the tropics.

BASKET STARS

Close relatives of the true brittle stars, basket stars tend to be bigger and have arms with many branches. These arms are even more flexible than those of brittle stars, although they are formed in a similar way. Basket stars are filter feeders. They trap their food by making a basket shape with their arms. The basket's "mouth" faces into the current.

Basket stars catch tiny prey with their arms.

DIFFERENT LIFESTYLES

Some brittle stars can live in brackish waters, an unusual ability for echinoderms. Most, however, live in the open ocean. They are common in shallow waters but even more abundant in the deep sea. In some places, they literally cover the sea bottom.

Most brittle stars are scavengers or feed on detritus—particles of food that drift down from above. Many, however, are also hunters, feeding on small worms and crustaceans. A few brittle stars are filter feeders, sifting plankton from the water.

SEA LILIES AND FEATHER STARS

When many people first see these animals, they mistake them for plants. Feather stars and sea lilies spend most of their lives quite still, waiting for their food to come to them.

ARMS AS NETS

Sea lilies and feather stars are filter feeders. They use their arms to sift out the tiny animals, algae, and other food suspended in the water. The fingerlike tube feet flick these particles into a central groove running down each arm. Microscopic hairlike structures called cilia then waft them down the base of the gutter toward the mouth at the animal's center.

HELD DOWN

Sea lilies spend their adult lives fixed to one spot. A stalk projecting from their bodies links them to the ocean floor. Like all echinoderms, as larvae, sea lilies swim free in the water column. Once they have started to mature, however, they settle, attaching themselves to rocks or other hard objects on the seafloor.

PREPARING TO FEED

At dusk, feather stars clamber to the tops of coral reefs and open their arms to capture passing plankton.

LITTLE LODGERS

Some creatures inhabit the arms of sea lilies and feather stars, picking off particles of food for themselves. Crustaceans, including certain shrimps and squat lobsters, live in this way, as does the tiny crinoid clingfish.

A crinoid squat lobster gathers food.

TANGLED LIMBS

Some sea lilies and feather stars have as many as 200 arms, which they use for feeding. Other species have as few as five.

FREE TO GO

Unlike sea lilies, feather stars have no stalk and can move very slowly. In shallow water, they often keep out of sight by day and travel to their feeding sites as night falls, unfurling the long arms surrounding their tiny bodies. Although they can move, feather stars rarely travel very far. Most spend their adult lives in one small area.

STEM AND PETALS

Sea lilies look like flowers. However, the resemblance is purely an accident of evolution.

CRINOID COLLECTIVE

Sea lilies and feather stars are sometimes known as crinoids. This is because they belong to the echinoderm class Crinoidea. There are around 625 known species in this class, although there may be many more. Sea lilies in particular are most common in the deep sea, much of which is still unexplored.

TINY BODY

Sea lilies and feather stars are almost all arms. Their bodies are often invisible, hidden behind or between the flamboyant limbs. At the center of the body is the mouth, which points upward.

DEFINING DIFFERENCES

Crinoids differ from other echinoderms in a number of ways. Although they have tube feet, which form the individual strands of the "feathers," these feet do not have suckers. Their arms are much more delicate and their bodies twisted so that both the mouth and exit hole face upward rather than toward the sea bottom.

Feather stars and sea lilies are far from rare, but their ancestors were much more widespread, occurring in such vast beds that they often outnumbered other marine organisms. Some ancient sea lilies were true giants, with stalks of well over 3 feet (.9 m) long.

SEA URCHINS

M ost people would agree that sea urchins are odd looking. Their mobile spines give them a unique appearance, and they have many other features that set them apart.

HARD CASE

A sea urchin's test is formed from interlocking plates of calcium carbonate. The same substance is produced by both crustaceans and mollusks to form their shells and hard body parts.

SPINY SKIN

The word *echinoderm* seems to fit sea urchins better than any of their relatives. It means spiny skin and spines are something sea urchins have in abundance. Some sea urchins have pointed spines to protect them from predators. Others have shorter, blunt spines, which they can use to wedge themselves safely into gaps between rocks.

TEST OF STRENGTH

Beneath the thin layer of skin from which a sea urchin's spines protrude is a tough, solid shell containing the animal's organs. This test is formed from plates of calcium carbonate that are welded together. As well as being strong, the test is lightweight and gives the sea urchin structure. Muscles that control and move the animal's spines attach to its solid surface.

LITTLE NIPPERS

As well as spines and tube feet, sea urchins have stalklike pedicellaria on their bodies. These are used to pick detritus off the skin and keep it free of parasites.

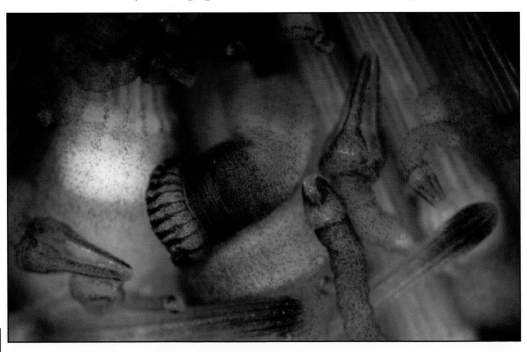

32

MOBILE MUNCHERS

Most sea urchins graze on algae. Some scrape films off these primitive, plantlike organisms from the seabed. Others feed on larger species of algae, the seaweeds. In places where their natural predators are scarce, sea urchins can become quite destructive. During the twentieth century, for example, they ravaged kelp forests along the Pacific coast of North America after their main predator there, the sea otter, was hunted close to extinction.

Although algae is the main diet of most sea urchins, they will turn to other food, including dead animal matter, if algae are scarce. In deep water, where there is no light for algae to grow, some sea urchins eat sponges and other simple animals.

NO WAY IN

Sea urchins are the best protected of all echinoderms. The long, sharp spines carried by many species keep predators away from their fleshy skin and delicate tube feet.

DUG OUT SHELTER

Some sea urchins that live in the tidal zone excavate holes using their sharp spines and teeth. These provide protection from the pounding waves and stop them from being washed away.

IN ONE END AND OUT THE OTHER

A sea urchin's mouth is on the bottom of its body. Inside the opening are "teeth" attached to hard plates controlled by a complex series of muscles. Food is drawn up into the stomach and travels around the intestine, where it is digested and the nutrients are absorbed. The waste is then ejected through the anus, or exit hole, on the top of the animal.

A top (dorsal) view of Hetrocentrotus mammilatus *showing its anus*

33

Although they all have the same basic structure, sea urchins vary, particularly in the shapes and sizes of their spines. Some species hide, but others are brightly colored. A few species are harmful to us.

BURST OF COLOR

This sea urchin belongs to the genus Diadema. Some Diadema species collect together in huge numbers on the seabed where food is plentiful.

MUSICAL SPINES

Pencil urchins have thick, hollow spines. In some places, they are becoming rare as people collect them to make their spines into wind chimes.

POINTED SPINES

There are around 950 known living sea urchin species. The most familiar are those with sharp, pointed spines. Edible sea urchins fall into this group, their spines offering little protection against the gloves of the divers who collect them. The spines of many sea urchins are poisonous. Both long- and short-spined species can inject poison via their spines. Some short-spined species can deliver poison without even breaking the skin of their victim.

The rough-spined sea urchin lives near Hawaii. It is also known as the Sputnik urchin since it resembles early satellites.

TINY SPINES

A few types of sea urchins hardly seem to have spines at all. The ball urchin, for instance, has tiny spines. It relies more on camouflage for defense, covering itself with shells and pieces of gravel to help it hide. Heart urchins plow through seabed sediment collecting particles of food with their tube feet. They also have very short spines to make burrowing easier.

BLUNT SPINES

Not all sea urchins have pointed spines. Some, such as the pencil urchins, have thick spines that end in blunt tips. Although these spines cannot puncture skin, they still help defend their owners. Pencil urchin spines contain a powerful irritant that is released when attacked.

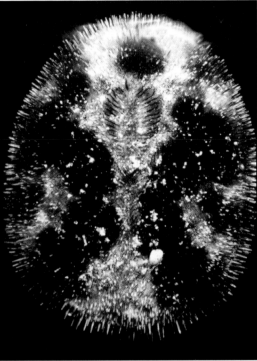

HEART URCHIN

There are many different species of heart urchins. This one comes from the Pacific Ocean. Heart urchins are often called sea potatoes because of their shape.

LITTLE DIGGER

This small Pacific species is a type of burrowing urchin. It uses its spines and "teeth" to dig burrows in soft rocks and reefs for protection.

SAND DOLLARS

Sand dollars have flattened, biscuit-shaped bodies covered with short spines. They live on top of, or partly buried in, sediment near the seashore. They feed by trapping particles of food from the water with sticky mucus.

Sand dollar tests are often found on beaches.

SEA CUCUMBERS

I f sea lilies are the animal equivalent of flowers, sea cucumbers are their vegetables. These weird creatures move so slowly across the seabed, they seem almost immobile.

UNIQUE APPEARANCE
In terms of their shape, sea cucumbers are well-named. These echinoderms have thick, elongated bodies with the mouth at one end and the exit hole at the other. Like all echinoderms, their bodies are built on a five-part plan, although it is difficult to see without cutting them open.

FEEDING FRONDS
The feeding tentacles of some sea cucumbers are finely branched for sifting plankton and other particles of food from the water.

ON THE SURFACE
Most sea cucumbers have two types of tube feet. Those around the mouth are adapted as tentacles and used in feeding. The rest have suckers and are spread across the underside of the body. These are used for movement. Sea cucumber skin is tough and often spiny. This makes them hard to kill and unpleasant to eat.

SLURPING SEDIMENTS
Some sea cucumbers are shorter and thicker than others. Like many, this species swallows sediment and digests the organic matter it contains.

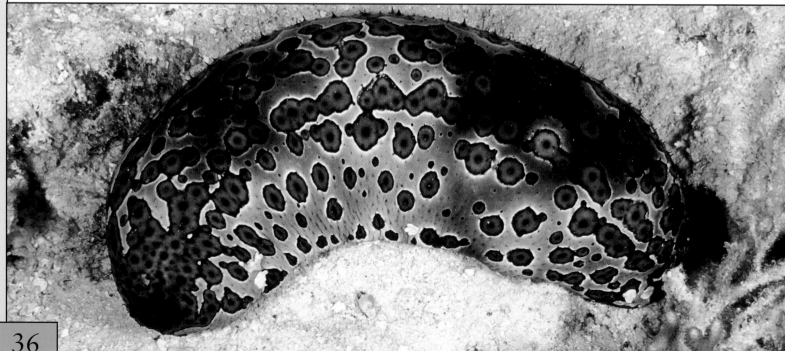

GREAT AND SMALL

Sea cucumbers make up the echinoderm class Holothuroidea. There are around 1,400 living species and they are found on the seabed, most commonly on and around coral reefs. Sea cucumbers vary greatly in size. The smallest are less than 1/2 of an inch (1 cm) long, and the largest can reach over 16 feet (5 m).

EXTRA DEFENSES

Sea cucumbers have thick, leathery skin. In most, this is filled with ossicles, or small disks, of calcium carbonate. Many species also have spines. A few sea cucumbers go one step further in defending themselves. They produce toxins that can be released through their skin to ward off, injure, or kill predators.

UNUSUAL ABODE

Pearlfish have perhaps the strangest homes in the animal kingdom. They spend their days inside the anal cavities of sea cucumbers. The relationship between the two animals is largely mysterious. Several species of pearlfish live in this way and scientists think some may eat the organs of the sea cucumber itself. Others emerge at night to feed in the waters around their host.

A pearlfish exits from its living hiding place.

ECHINODERM RELATIVES

Despite their often simple external appearances, echinoderms have many internal structures in common with more complex animals. Their closest relatives fill the gap between vertebrates and invertebrates.

HEMICHORDATA

Hemichordates are not much to look at and few people have heard of them. However, they are hugely important in terms of evolution. Hemichordates bridge the divide between invertebrate animals and chordates, creatures that have a notocord or supporting spinal rod. Their closest invertebrate relatives are the echinoderms. This relationship can be seen in their larvae, which look very similar to those of some echinoderms.

Hemichordates have a body divided into three parts: the preoral lobe (at the front), the collar, and the trunk. They have two simple structures that resemble true notocords and these show their close relationship to the chordates.

SEA SQUIRT

Adult sea squirts suspension-feed by pumping water through their baglike bodies.

CHORDATA

This phylum in animal classification is split into three smaller groups, known as subphyla. One contains all the vertebrate classes: fish, amphibians, reptiles, birds, and mammals. Another contains the cephalochordates, or lancelets. The third subphylum, Tunicata, has three separate classes: these contain sea squirts, larvaceans, and salps.

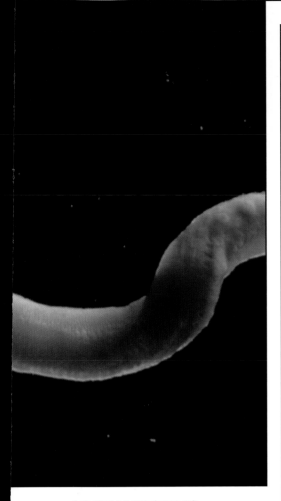

LANCELETS

Lancelets are the most fishlike of nonvertebrate chordates. They live in warm and temperate seas, burying themselves in sand until only their heads are visible. Lancelets feed by pumping water into their mouths and through their sievelike gill slits, which remove any edible particles. They sometimes leave their hiding places and swim by sending waves through the muscular blocks in their bodies. Lancelets lack eyes and jaws but retain their notocord for their whole life.

Most lancelets are less than 3 inches (75 mm) long.

ACORN WORMS

There are only around 100 known species of hemichordate. Most are acorn worms, which inhabit marine sediment. The rest are pterobranchs that build tubes to live in the seabed.

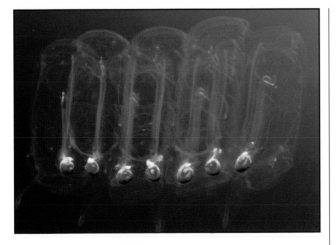

CIRCLE OF LIFE

Some salps form ring-shaped colonies (above). Others join together in huge colonial chains.

TUNICATES

The stiff notocord of sea squirts is only present in their larvae, which resemble tadpoles. It supports the body like a backbone does in vertebrates, but it is lost as the animal matures and settles into its sedentary life stuck to rocks.

Salps resemble sea squirts, but they float freely in the water column as adults, often forming large colonies. They also have larvae that resemble tadpoles, losing their notocord as they develop. Larvaceans are almost too small to see with the naked eye. They hunt plankton in open water.

A lthough echinoderms are invertebrates, many grow to be quite large. The chalky plates in their skin help to strengthen their bodies and the water in which they live supports their weight.

BIG AND TOUGH

Some sea cucumbers grow to be thicker than a man's thigh. Being large makes them safer. The bigger an echinoderm is, the fewer predators are able to kill it.

QUITE A HANDFUL

Several starfish reach large sizes. Like all echinoderms, they continue growing throughout their lifetime, although the rate of growth slows down as they get older.

SEA MONSTERS

Echinoderms include some of the largest of all invertebrates. The longest sea cucumber, *Synapta maculata*, can grow to more than 10 feet (3 m) long. Although shorter, some other sea cucumbers are even thicker and more massive than this species. The species *Thelenota anax*, which also lives in the Pacific Ocean, grows to more than 3 feet (.9 m) long and can be 9 1/2 inches (24 cm) wide.

SPINY GIANTS

The world's largest sea urchins live in deep water off the coast of Japan. Known only by their Latin name *Sperosoma giganteum*, these spiny monsters have an average test diameter of 1 foot (30 cm). Another deep sea species, *Hygrosoma hoplacantha,* is almost as big. Both have flexible tests that look like flying saucers and collapse if brought to the surface.

Sperosoma giganteum

MEGA STARS

Although not as long as the biggest sea cucumbers, some starfish become giants, too. *Midgardia xandaros*, which lives in the Gulf of Mexico, can have an arm span of 4 1/2 feet (1.38 m). Its many arms are long but very slender. Much heavier is the five-armed starfish *Thromidia catalai*, which lives off New Caledonia. It can weigh more than 13 pounds (6 kg).

LIFE IN MINIATURE

Some echinoderms are very small. The smallest echinoderm of all is a sea cucumber, *Psammothuria ganapatii*. It grows to a maximum length of just 3/20 of an inch (4 mm). *Echinocyamus scaber* is the smallest sea urchin, with a test diameter of 1/4 of an inch (6 mm). The smallest starfish, *Patiriella parvivipara*, grows to just 1/5 of an inch (5 mm) across.

LARGER THAN LIFE

Some starfish are easily overlooked. Many, such as the ones shown enlarged above, are smaller than a child's fingernail.

41

Most humans have little contact with living echinoderms. We inhabit land, whereas they live in the sea. However, people kill and collect echinoderms for several reasons.

SOLD AS SOUVENIRS

Starfish are gathered and dried in large numbers to be sold to tourists at seaside resorts. Sea urchin tests also find their way into souvenir shops, although they are normally collected when washed up on beaches, their original owners already long dead. Pencil urchins, however, are caught alive and killed for their spines.

OUT TO DRY

These starfish have been collected to be sold to tourists. Although this activity has little effect on global echinoderm numbers, it can cause small, localized populations to collapse.

MEDICAL APPLICATIONS

Echinoderms have long been used in traditional Chinese medicine. Research is now showing that they may have applications in conventional Western medicine, too. Proteins isolated from sea cucumbers have been found to be effective against cancer cells. In time, these creatures may provide new anti-cancer drugs. Trials are also under way to test the effectiveness of the sea cucumber proteins against viral diseases, including HIV/AIDS.

Collecting sea urchins has become big business, employing 12,000 people in California and Maine.

CAUGHT FOR FOOD

Few people in Europe or North America eat echinoderms but in Asia all sorts of species appear on the menu. Sea urchin roe is particularly popular in Japan, where it is eaten raw as a kind of sushi. The sea urchins of California that were once considered pests are now collected for sale in the Japanese market.

FARMING ECHINODERMS

Sea cucumbers are also eaten in Japan, as well as in China and other countries in Asia. Several species are gathered and dried out for preparation as food. Collectively, these edible sea cucumbers are known as trepang.

In many parts of Asia, sea cucumbers are collected to be sold. However, this puts pressure on wild populations, so some people have begun farming the creatures instead. In Japan, sea cucumber farming has become quite successful and techniques have been developed to farm sea urchins, too.

The Japanese enjoy eating sea urchin roe, which they call "uni." Recently, demand has become so great that they have started importing it from abroad.

Sea cucumbers could save human lives.

Sea otters were hunted close to extinction for their beautiful fur. As their numbers dropped, the population of sea urchins exploded.

ANIMAL CLASSIFICATION

The animal kingdom can be split into two main groups, vertebrates (with a backbone) and invertebrates (without a backbone). From these two main groups, scientists classify, or sort, animals further based on their shared characteristics.

The six main groupings of animals, from the most general to the most specific, are: phylum, class, order, family, genus, and species. This system was created by Carolus Linnaeus.

To see how this system works, follow the example of how human beings are classified in the vertebrate group and how earthworms are classified in the invertebrate group.

ANIMAL KINGDOM

VERTEBRATE

PHYLUM: Chordata

CLASS: Mammals

ORDER: Primates

FAMILY: Hominids

GENUS: *Homo*

SPECIES: *sapiens*

INVERTEBRATE

PHYLUM: Annelida

CLASS: Oligochaeta

ORDER: Haplotaxida

FAMILY: Lumbricidae

GENUS: *Lumbricus*

SPECIES: *terrestris*

There are more than 30 groups of phyla. The nine most common are listed below along with their common name.

Annelida
(SEGMENTED WORMS)

Arthropoda
(ARTHROPODS)

Chordata
(CHORDATES)

Cnidaria
(CNIDARIANS)

ECHINODERMATA
(ECHINODERMS)

Mollusca
(MOLLUSKS)

Nematoda
(ROUNDWORMS)

Platyhelminthes
(FLATWORMS)

Porifera
(SPONGES)

This book highlights animals from the Echinodermata phylum. Follow the example below to learn how scientists classify the *Arbacia punctulata*, or the purple-spined sea urchin.

INVERTEBRATE

PHYLUM: Echinodermata

CLASS: Echinoidea

ORDER: Arbacioida

FAMILY: Arbaciidae

GENUS: *Arbacia*

SPECIES: *punctulata*

Arbacia punctulata
(Purple-spined sea urchin)

GLOSSARY

ALGAE
Simple plantlike organisms that survive by photosynthesis

EVOLUTION
The process by which new animals appear and change over time

EXTINCT
Died out; once a species has become extinct, it has gone forever

FOSSIL
The preserved remains of an animal or an impression in rock

FRONDS
Leaflike organ formed by stem and foliage

GILLS
Structures used by animals to remove oxygen from water

GONADS
Organs that produce eggs or sperm

HABITAT
The area or type of environment in which an animal naturally occurs

HYDRAULIC
Operated by water pressure in contained pipes or tubes

INVERTEBRATE
An animal without a backbone or spinal cord

LARVA
An animal's young, immature body form before it becomes an adult

PALEONTOLOGIST
A scientist who studies organisms that are now extinct

PARASITE
An animal that lives on or inside another animal, feeding on it while giving back nothing in return

PEDICELLARIA
Appendages on the skin of some echinoderms, used for defense, removing parasites, or collecting particles of food

PHOTOSYNTHESIS
The process by which algae and plants use the energy from sunlight to create food

PLANKTON
Tiny animals and other living organisms that live suspended in water

PREDATOR
An animal that hunts others for food

PREY
An animal that is hunted by a predator

PROTEINS
Complex chemicals produced by animals and used by them to make body tissues and other natural substances

REPRODUCTION
The process by which a new generation of animals is created

SCAVENGER
An animal that feeds on carrion

SEDIMENT
Mud, sand, or other particles that settle on the sea bottom

SUSPENSION FEEDER
An animal that sifts its food from water

Look for more Animal Kingdom books:

Tree Frogs, Mud Puppies & Other Amphibians
ISBN 0-7565-1249-2

Ant Lions, Wasps & Other Insects
ISBN 0-7565-1250-6

Peacocks, Penguins & Other Birds
ISBN 0-7565-1251-4

Angelfish, Megamouth Sharks & Other Fish
ISBN 0-7565-1252-2

Bats, Blue Whales & Other Mammals
ISBN 0-7565-1249-2

Centipedes, Millipedes, Scorpions & Spiders
ISBN 0-7565-1254-9

Dwarf Geckos, Rattlesnakes & Other Reptiles
ISBN 0-7565-1255-7

Snails, Shellfish & Other Mollusks
ISBN 0-7565-1613-7

Lobsters, Crabs & Other Crustaceans
ISBN 0-7565-1612-9

Nematodes, Leeches & Other Worms
ISBN 0-7565-1615-3

Sponges, Jellyfish & Other Simple Animals
ISBN 0-7565-1614-5

FURTHER RESOURCES

AT THE LIBRARY

Blaxland, Beth. *Sea Stars, Sea Urchins, and Their Relatives: Echinoderms.* Philadelphia: Chelsea House Publications, 2002.

Hirschmann, Kris. *Sea Urchins.* San Diego: KidHaven Press, 2005.

Sullivan, Jody. *Sea Stars.* San Diego: Kid Haven Press, 2005.

Svancara, Theresa. *Sea Stars and Other Echinoderms.* Chicago: World Book Inc., 2002.

On the Web
For more information on *echinoderms*, use FactHound to track down Web sites related to this book.
1. Go to *www.facthound.com*
2. Type in a search word related to this book or this book ID: 0756516110
3. Click on the *Fetch It* button FactHound will find the best Web sites for you.